ABC Vegetables

A Bilingual Reversible Book!

by Michelle Marcotte and Joël Beddows

Wonderful vegetables are highlighted in this reversible English and French book that is easy to read aloud by parents and grandparents – even in the other language. Intended to assist adult and child language learning, it will also spark interest in exploring a wide variety of vegetables.

Contact Michelle Marcotte
Books:
https://www.michellemarcottebooks.com Art: https://www.michellemarcotte.com

Archway Publishing books may be ordered through booksellers or by contacting:

Archway Publishing
1663 Liberty Drive
Bloomington, IN 47403
www.archwaypublishing.com
844-669-3957

ISBN: 978-1-6657-3446-2 (sc)
ISBN: 978-1-6657-3445-5 (e)

Print information available on the last page.

Archway Publishing rev. date: 01/26/2023

For Raphaëlle, Maxwell, Julia and Hannah,
our children who eat well.

The authors thank Lisa Langer, owner of Pencil in the River Studios, North Tonawanda New York for fine art photography.

A

is for artichoke
– prickly on the outside but
soft on the inside.

B
is for beautiful,
sweet beets.

C is for cabbage lovely in green or purple.

D is for crisp and delicious daikon radish.

E is for eggplant

– it isn't an egg at all!
(une aubergine)

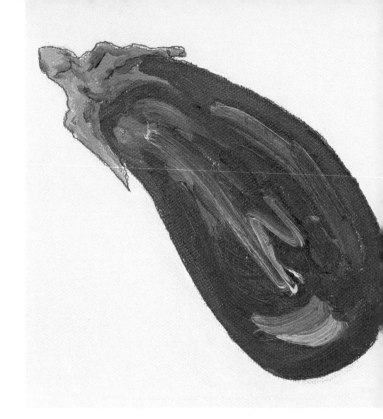

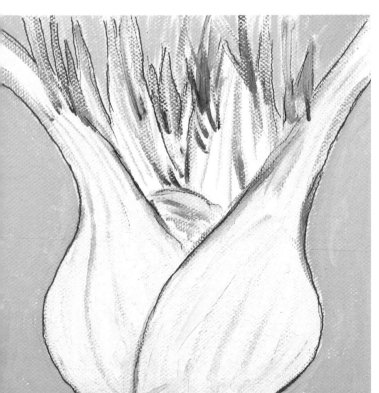

F is for fennel

– a vegetable that tastes
like licorice.

G
is for healthy and pungent garlic.

H
is for habanero pepper

– a little gives a big hot taste. (piment habanero)

I is for mild and crisp iceberg lettuce.

(laitue iceberg)

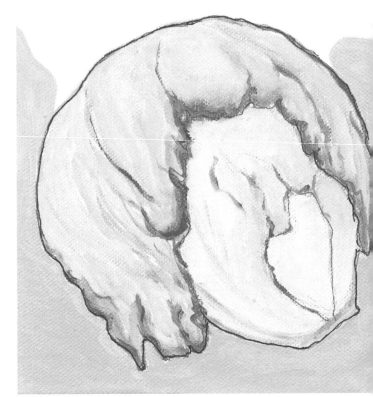

J is for jalapeno pepper

– so terrific with Mexican flavours.

K

is for versatile kale

– cook it with garlic or blend it in a smoothie.
(le chou frisé)

L

is for leeks

– luscious flavour for pies or soups.
(le poireaux)

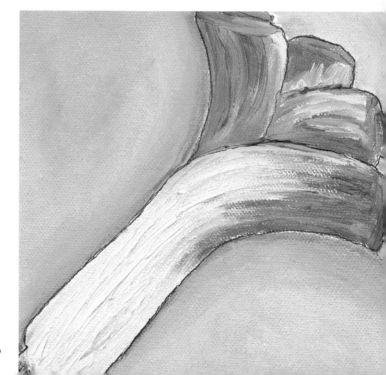

M is for mushrooms

– put some in your omelette.
(les champignons)

N is for nasturtium

– an edible orange flower with leaves that taste peppery.
(la capuchine)

O is for onions

- long and green or gold and round, they flavour everything.

P is for plantains
the vegetable that looks like a banana.

Q is for quiche cooked with asparagus or broccoli.

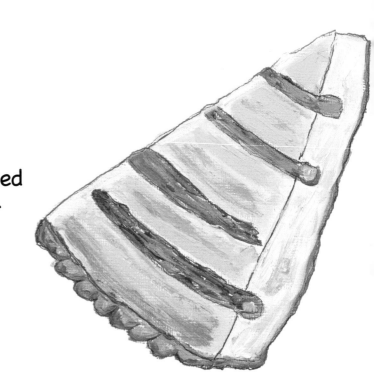

R is for radish

– the first vegetable in your spring garden.

S is for so many different squashes. (la courge)

T is for tomato a bright flavor and color whether fresh in salads or cooked in sauces.

U
— yoU can pick vegetables!

V
is for victory when you eat vegetables.

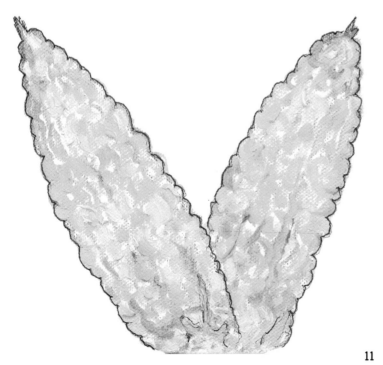

W

is for watercress a delightfully peppery flavor with butter in a sandwich. (le cresson)

X

— eXtra Vegetables Please!

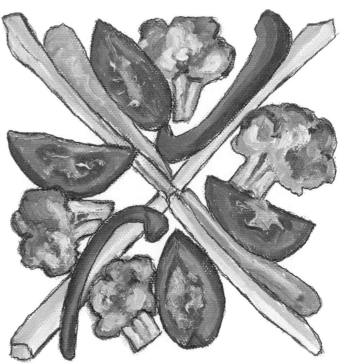

12

Y is for yucca to make crispy fries.

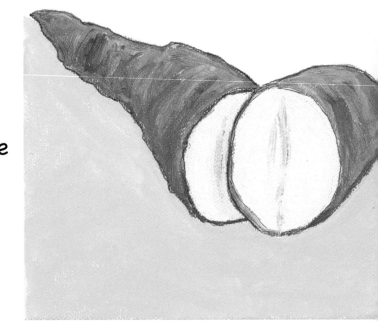

Z is for zinnia, an edible flower grown by astronauts on the space station.

Michelle Marcotte, co-author and illustrator is an award-winning painter, author,

terrific cook, international agri-environmental regulatory consultant, loving mother and grandmother. Michelle's happy memories speaking French to her grandparents led to a lifelong devotion (and struggle) to speak French (and to eating well!)

Photo credit : Craig Fallis

Joël Beddows, co-author, is a professor at the Department of Theatre, Faculty of

Arts, University of Ottawa, where he is also Special Councilor for Francophone Affairs to the Dean. Joël is an award-winning theatre director, artistic director, academic, author and translator (in English and French) and the loving father to a charming, bilingual daughter.

Photo credit : Maude Chauvin

Printed in the United States
by Baker & Taylor Publisher Services

Abécédaire
des légumes

Livre bilingue réversible!

de Michelle Marcotte et Joël Beddows

Cet abécédaire se veut une invitation aux parents et aux grands-parents de partager le monde des légumes – même dans une langue seconde. Il a été rédigé avec l'espoir de faciliter la découverte des légumes inusités.

Contact Michelle Marcotte
Livres:
https://www.michellemarcottebooks.com De l'art: https://www.michellemarcotte.com

Il il peut être commandé auprès des libraires ou :

Archway Publishing
1663 Liberty Drive
Bloomington, IN 47403
www.archwaypublishing.com
844-669-3957

ISBN: 978-1-6657-3446-2 (sc)
ISBN: 978-1-6657-3445-5 (e)

Print information available on the last page.

Archway Publishing rev. date: 01/26/2023

Á Raphaëlle, Maxwell, Julia et Hannah,
nos enfants qui mangent bien.

Les auteurs tiennent à remercie Lisa Langer, propriétaire
de Pencil in the Rivers Studios, North Tonawanda
New York pour les excellentes photographies.

A
comme artichaut

– une belle fleur verte avec un cœur tendre.

B
comme betteraves

– belles, rondes et sucrées.

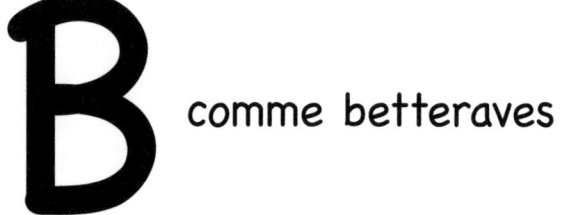

1

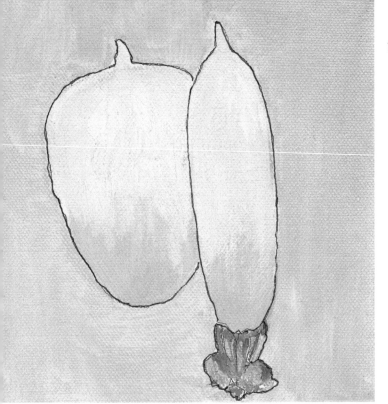

D comme radis daikon

– un radis blanc
croustillant et délicieux.

C comme chou

– qu'il soit vert ou violet.

E comme endive

– délicieuse dans une salade avec du fromage et des noix. (Endive is also called chicory.)

F comme fenouil

– un légume qui goûte l'anis.

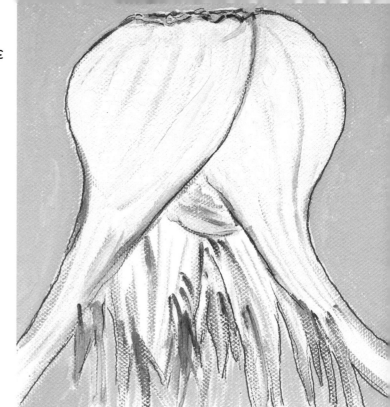

G comme gingembre

– une racine exotique et bonne pour la santé.
(ginger root)

H comme haricots, verts, jaunes or en fèves.
(beans)

I
comme igname

– si important pour la cuisine africaine.
(yams)

J
comme piment jalapeno

– très utilisé dans la cuisine mexicaine.

K comme kilogramme.

Pouvez - vous manger un kilo de légumes chaque semaine?
(Can you eat a kilogram of vegetables each week?)

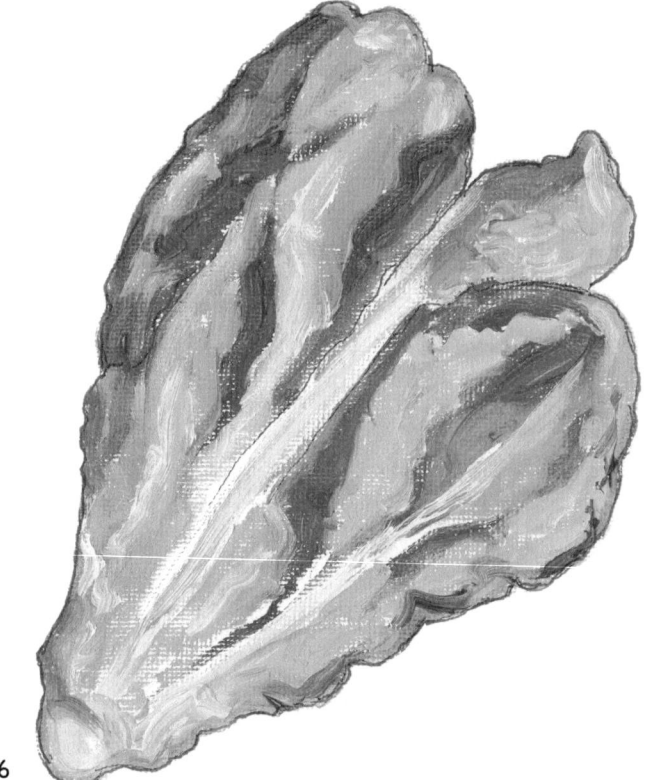

L comme laitue

– une belle salade à manger avec un filet d'huile d'olive. (lettuce)

6

M comme maïs

– à manger à la fin d'été.
(corn)

N comme navet

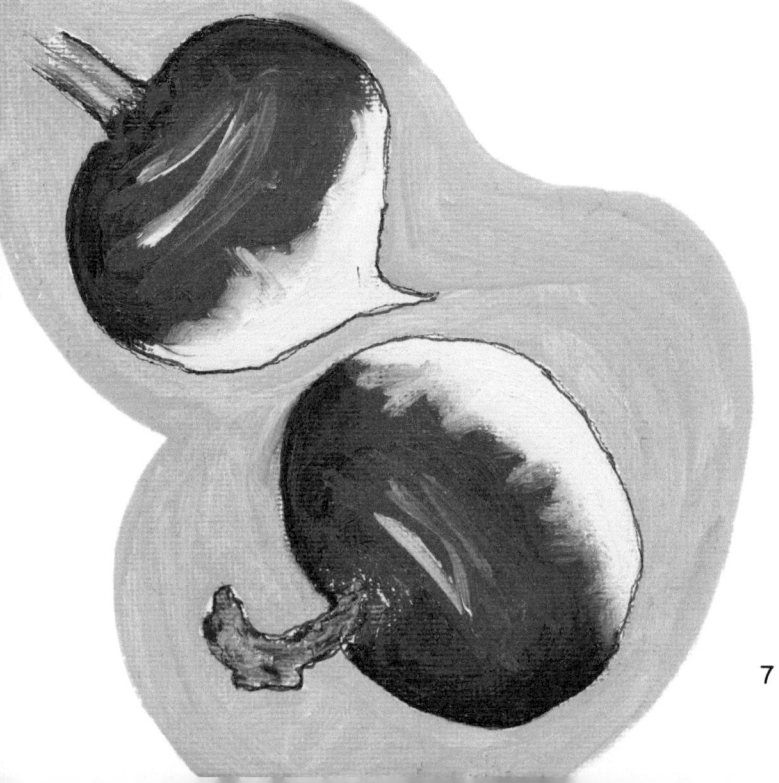

– aromatisé au beurre et
à la muscade.
(turnip)

O comme oignon

- long et vert ou rond et jaune ou blanc. Ils donnent de la saveur à tous vos plats!

P comme plantains

– un légume qui ressemble à une banane.

8

Q comme quiche

– qu'elle soit aux asperges ou au brocoli.

R comme radis

– le premier légume qui pousse dans votre jardin le printemps.

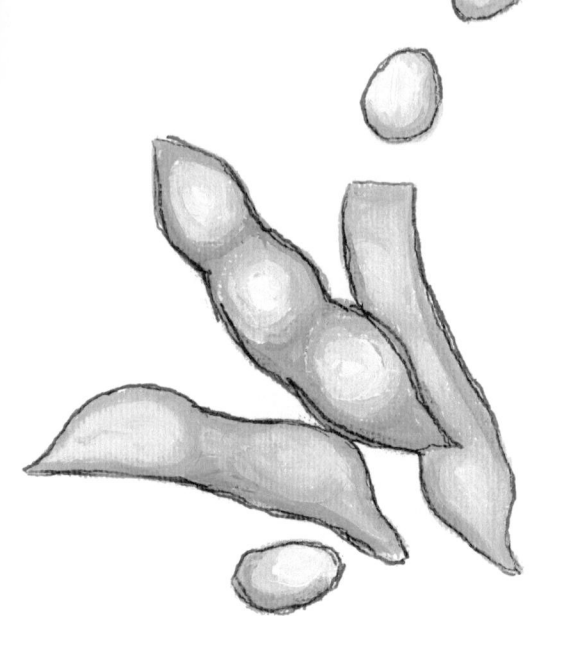

S comme soja

– à cuire comme collation ou à inclure dans une salade.
(Soya beans are also called edamame.)

T comme tomate

– savoureuse et colorée à manger soit fraiche dans les salades ou cuite dans les sauces.

Très  tile pour ta santé.

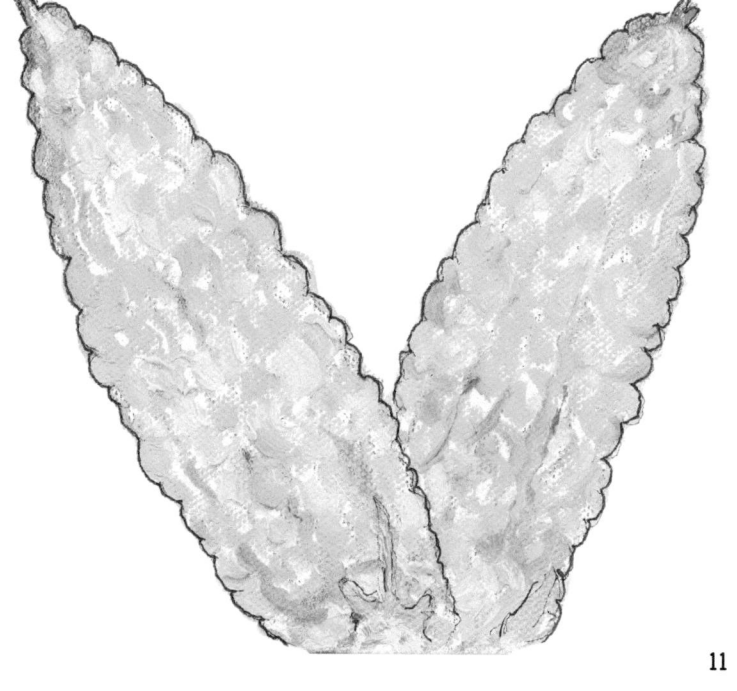

Le V de la victoire

– quand vous mangez vos légumes.

11

W

comme wasabi

– à manger avec votre sushi.
(Wasabi flavors sushi.)

X

— Xoxo comme les bisous et les câlins aussitôt que tu as terminé tes légumes.
(Kisses and hugs when you eat your vegetables.)

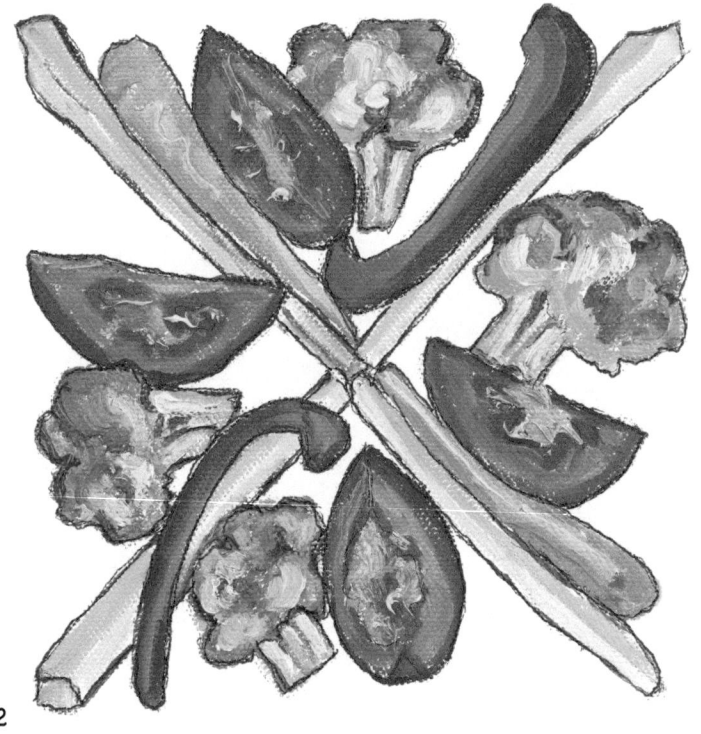

Y comme yucca

– qui font des frites croustillantes.

Z comme zinnia

– une fleur comestible cultivée par les astronautes dans la station spatiale.

Michelle Marcotte est une artiste peintre primée, une écrivaine de langue anglaise, une formidable cuisinière, une consultante internationale en réglementation agroenvironnementale, une mère et grand-mère aimante. Elle se rappelle d'avoir parlé français avec ses propres grands-parents, ce qui a nourri son propre désir de partager cette langue (et de bien manger).

Photo Credit : Craig Fallis

Joël Beddows est un professeur agrégé au Département de théâtre de la Faculté des Arts, Université d'Ottawa, ainsi que conseiller en francophonie au décanat de cette même faculté. Il a mis en scène de nombreuses productions primées, tout en œuvrant en tant que directeur artistique, chercheur, auteur et traducteur (en anglais et en français). Il est aussi le fier papa d'une fille charmante et bilingue.

Photo credit : Maude Chauvin